THE ILLUSTRATED COTTAGE

A DECORATIVE FAIRY TALE INSPIRED BY PROVENCE

NIÑA WILLIAMS

A COUNTRY LIVING Book

Photographs by
KEITH SCOTT MORTON

Murals and Illustrations by
BARB FISHER AND LAURA CHAPPELL

HEARST BOOKS
A Division of Sterling Publishing Co., Inc.
NEW YORK

PHOTO CREDITS
Michael Drejza: pages 2-3, 68, 100, 108, 110-111, 112-113, 116-117 (except top right)
Niña Williams: pages v, 107, 109, 114, 126 (left, right), 134
Jessie Walker: pages 4, 126 (middle)

Garlic Rabbit recipe by Richard Olney. *From Lulu's Provençal Table: The Exuberant Food and Wine from the Domaine Tempier Vineyard.* Published by HarperCollins Publishers. Copyright © 1994 by Richard Olney. This usage granted by permission of Lescher & Lescher, Ltd.

BOOK DESIGN BY SUSI OBERHELMAN, SVO GRAPHIC DESIGN
Library of Congress Cataloging-in-Publication Data
Available upon request.

10 9 8 7 6 5 4 3 2 1

First Paperback Edition 2003
Published by Hearst Books
A Division of Sterling Publishing Co., Inc.
387 Park Avenue South, New York, NY 10016

www.countryliving.com

Distributed in Canada by Sterling Publishing
c/o Canadian Manda Group, One Atlantic Avenue, Suite 105
Toronto, Ontario, Canada M6K 3E7
Distributed in Australia by Capricorn Link (Australia) Pty. Ltd.
P.O. Box 704, Windsor, NSW 2756 Australia

Manufactured in China

ISBN 1-58816-239-7

TO MY BELOVED DAUGHTERS,

RACHEL AND ANA,

WHO WILL ALWAYS LIVE IN

The Illustrated Cottage

CONTENTS

Foreword   viii

Introduction   I

SÉVERINE   The Foyer   9

ROBERT   The Salon   17

MAURICE   The Dining Room   31

CÉLESTE   The Kitchen   41

DELPHINE   The Atelier   53

NIÑA   The Boudoir   69

ARIANE   The Carriage House   81

FLORA   The Garden   101

Bibliography   120

Acknowledgments   126

Index   129

Foreword

The Illustrated Cottage, Provence, Niña Williams . . . where does one end and another begin? This delicious book you are about to savor, like Niña the person, is a treasure chest of surprises, experiences, fantasy, romance, and, yes, practical information. If ever a book could serve as a testament to the inventiveness of its author, this is it. I've known and worked with Niña Williams for more than twenty-seven years, from our first meeting at *American Home* magazine through our decades together at *Country Living* to her visionary creation of *Country Living Gardener* magazine. Through the years I've continuously marveled at her ability to celebrate and capture the beauty of nature, architecture, and design for her editorial pages. But it is even more wondrous to witness Niña's ability to *create* beauty and uniqueness from the germ of an idea.

When Niña first told me she was going to transform her new home into an experience of Provence (with no firsthand knowledge of the place) I said to myself, "Only Niña would attempt that." And when she spoke of her dream to produce this book with its concurrent themes, I judged the task even more daunting.

But here we are with a charming love story, a travelogue, a decorating manual, and a history lesson. A team of talented professionals, starting with mural artists Barb Fisher and Laura Chappell and photographer Keith Scott Morton, under Niña's direction, have given us a visual banquet. Layers of Provençal culture and decorative style have been woven into a seamless panorama of romance. But it is the unexpected presence of historical background, design details, and practical how-to information that make *The Illustrated Cottage* unique and render it an invaluable handbook for anyone who, like Niña, loves all things Provençal, or who simply loves their home.

RACHEL NEWMAN

Editor Emerita, *Country Living*

Introduction

If the decoration of a house may be considered a form of autobiography, then my illustrated cottage may be called an apt reflection of my life. Although in real life I have never been to the region in southern France called Provence, my story is intimately bound up with its spirit and character, its colors and landscape. For Provence is a place I can smell and taste in my dreams, an Eden of wild rocky promontories and lapis-blue fields, filled with the pungent scents and flavors of fresh lavender and garlic. It is a place I have roamed many times in my mind. Because it is so much a part of me, Provence—and French design in general—is a vehicle to tell my story, to express my imagination and realize what I see with my mind's eye.

Fascinated with color and visual stimulation from an early age, I have pursued a long career as a design editor for books and magazines. I seek out homes, gardens, and collections to photograph or in which to create a particular scene—from scratch, when necessary. I have never lost the thrill of documenting other people's accomplishments through the medium of photography, and in effect capturing an individual story for leisurely contemplation forever.

As a young art student, I was enamored of painting, and although I was an adept draftsman, the craft necessary to translate from nature the colors I wished to lay on canvas eluded me. My preoccupation with painting persisted, however, and in my studies I was introduced to the witticisms of trompe l'oeil. Literally translated, this French term means "fool the eye." A method of making an artwork closely resemble a real environment, trompe l'oeil has a long, rich tradition in art and decoration. One of the earliest extant examples is a second-century Roman mosaic by Heracleitus called *The Unswept Floor*. It depicts a floor covered with scraps of refuse, leaves, and half-eaten chicken legs, and even includes a mouse, all given a marvelous degree of perspective and realism by the skillful rendition of sharply etched shadows. Egyptian tomb paintings, Pompeiian murals, Italian frescoes, even Japanese screens have contributed to the evolution of trompe l'oeil by creating illusions of actual space and figures within domestic dwellings and public buildings. Whether the scenes recount myths and legends or record historic, religious, and seasonal events, trompe l'oeil has often afforded them greater drama and impact.

Probably the strongest influence on the decoration of my own cottage has been exerted by Carl Larsson (1853–1919), a Swedish illustrator and painter famous for the vibrant and imaginative decorative painting of his house in the village of Sundborn and for his idyllic pictures of his wife and many children within domestic settings. The presence of color and beauty in his own home was as vital to Larsson as breath itself.

All of these precedents and the collaboration of talented trompe l'oeil artists Barb Fisher

and Laura Chappell helped me to conceive the painted designs in the illustrated cottage. In the realm of the cottage, I tossed aside the limitations of geography and circumstance and allowed a deep need to become rooted to a place I loved rule the scheme. I planned the decoration from several points of view: house as autobiography; house as dream; house as fairy tale; and house as French fantasy. Here I should state vehemently that the cottage is far from being a purist statement on French and Provençal design. Although some elements are French, the furnishings throughout are an extremely eclectic, personal gathering of art, antiques, and objects from all over the world assembled to *suggest* a story set in Provence.

Within the framework of the murals painted by Barb Fisher and Laura Chappell, the cottage becomes an illustrated book, a series of scenes from the pages of a travel journal portraying beloved people and places from the past. More specifically, the trompe l'oeil paintings represent the memories of my imagined alter ego, Delphine, a French-American girl who travels as an adolescent to Provence in 1918 to visit her aunt and uncle. The family lives outside of Sault, a village in the Vaucluse, the northwestern *département* of Provence, an area particularly suited for the cultivation of lavender. Delphine's first memory of the trip is the sight of her cousin, beautiful fourteen-year-old Séverine, reading a mysterious letter at the window of a Provençal *mas,* or farmhouse. The *mas* is located on Séverine's parents' country estate, a lavender farm, and the succeeding murals are images from Delphine's annual summer visits to see her cousins Séverine and Ariane. Although every effort has been made to base the fairy tale in accurate historical fact (market day in Sault, for example, allegedly has occurred on Wednesday for more than five hundred years), we do assume poetic license in some aspects of the murals; for instance, plants that do not normally bloom at the same time in Provence, like poppies and lavender, might be shown flowering together to capture an idealized essence of the place.

The illustrated cottage, actually built in 1936, is set and decorated in the style of that era, when Delphine, now an artist, paints the Provençal scenes from her childhood on the walls of her

American home. These "postcards from Provence" are really symbolic of a province in the heart and in the mind's eye. The unifying motif of lavender in each of the murals provides the Proustian trigger for all Delphine's memories. The furnishings of the cottage also reflect an eccentric gypsy-like spirit, the expression of a traveler who has layered souvenirs of her journeys with panache and appreciation; the exuberant mélange of colors, styles, and periods is a statement of artistic individuality and emancipation. Lots of touches augment the French and Provençal themes: the collection of rustic antique and vintage furniture, old chandeliers, candles of every hue and shape, worn tole trays, elegant flower arrangements, dressmaker-like swags of curtains and vintage laces. I did not select furnishings and artworks because of their fine quality or provenance as valuable antiques or objects. Rather, I chose them because of their direct sentimental character and aesthetic appeal.

The order in which the characters were painted do not reflect the chronological narration of the fairy tale. Indeed, the story unfolded and became clear in an almost mystical fashion for me, Barb, and Laura as the murals were painted. Céleste, the peasant woman harvesting lavender, came first, followed by the panorama of the lavender fields. Feeling that Céleste needed a companion, we designed Maurice, who drinks red wine as Céleste labors. Séverine and Ariane, the protagonists and daughters of the lavender estate, followed. And finally Delphine, the bohemian artist, appeared to give raison d'être to the tale. Ultimately, the paintings are both decorative and allegorical—depictions of romantic settings with strong botanical symbolism, and because the story is a fantasy with some roots in reality (Séverine and Ariane are really my own daughters, Rachel and Ana), the cottage invents its own history, a "trompe l'oeil history" of sorts.

Who can explain the nurturing, sustaining, and inspiring role art plays in all our lives? Perhaps it is the dream-like quality of art, and thus its ability to engender ideas, that makes art's presence so important. Finally, if fairy tales imply wishes and convey morals, I would hope that *The Illustrated Cottage* fulfills a universal wish for beauty and teaches the celebration of love.

SÉVERINE

Once upon a time, a French girl, about fourteen years of age, lived in an old stone cottage, or *mas*, near the Provençal town of Sault. The child, Séverine, relished inhaling the pungent scents of lavender fields crisscrossing her parents' farm. She plucked cherries and plums from the sunstruck orchards beneath the chalky summit of Mont Ventoux, and she hid in the oak woods where farm pigs rooted for black truffles in winter. Each Wednesday, when her family took great bunches of fresh lavender to market in town, the girl spent a few cents for a handful of honey nougat; then she would run with her sister and cousin to watch the boys play a game of *boules*. A youth called Robert noticed Séverine's skin was as creamy as white nougat, her hair as yellow as spring-flowering broom. Back at the cottage, Séverine dreamed that the broad-shouldered boy who laughed at the children's antics might someday ask to walk with her in her parents' garden. One afternoon, the postman delivered a basket brimming with blush roses. Tucked among the petals was a letter tied with lilac ribbon.

THE
Foyer

WHEN I HAPPENED UPON
my cottage a few years ago, I was on the brink
of a new life—a reinvention of home was necessary. Gypsy-like, I had traveled from house to
house, and this time I yearned to make the
cottage the retreat of a wanderer come to rest. I
wished for coziness, for stacks of books, for a lay-
ering of intensely personal allusions, for a spirit
of sensuous playfulness and fun.

I resolved to work with two old friends
and colleagues, trompe l'oeil artists Barb Fisher
and Laura Chappell, to set a convincing *mise-
en-scène*. I admired their talent, sensitivity to color,
and technical abilities. Additionally, they possessed
a knack for incorporating historical accuracy
into their designs as well as whimsy and humor.
In short, they were the perfect team to illustrate

The mural of Séverine (opposite)
sets the tone for the Provençal fairy tale.
A spirited palette of rich reds and
teals welcomes visitors into the foyer and stair
hall, where a weathered 1930s French wicker
bistro chair and a collection of turn-of-the-
century French walking sticks bear witness
to owners and stories gone by. (Above)
Lavender is the leitmotif of all the murals.

the cottage, to imbue it with the fanciful and childlike beauty of a fairy tale.

The word foyer derives from the Old French *foier*, for fireplace, from the Latin *focus*, for hearth. The entry to the cottage aptly describes the warm heart of the story. Its mural provides the starting point for mapping a woman's journey and for expressing my philosophy of the cottage as a metaphor for imagination.

As the viewer enters the hall, he looks simultaneously into the window of an old Provençal farmhouse, really a trompe l'oeil mural painted by Fisher and Chappell. Séverine reads her first love letter, although her calm demeanor and

The foyer mural separates the entrance from the salon beyond. Exuberant sprays of blush-pink climbing roses frame the window of Séverine's cottage, where rough-hewn shutters and stone sill and arch evoke the charming architectural elements of a rustic Provençal mas. *Behind brocade and lace curtains, pensive young Séverine contemplates a mysterious letter.*

French Farmhouses

RURAL HOMES in France are built with materials at hand, and Provençal houses, in particular, reflect Roman and Mediterranean influences with their local rubble and ashlar stone walls and their unglazed terra-cotta canal tile roofs. The archetypal country house, called a *mas*, is a long squat structure with a low-pitched one-angled or hipped roof. Limestone, sandstone, clay, oak, chestnut, beech, and poplar are traditional materials. Often, the *mas* incorporates a barn or, variously, sheep pens, stables, pigsties, and dovecotes, and the compound faces southeast to shelter from the effects of the bitter northwesterly wind, the mistral. The north side of the house rarely has windows, and windows are kept small on the south to keep the house cool during hot, dry summers. The residence is usually divided into the *salle*, or kitchen with living room, and the *chambres*, or bedrooms.

smooth coiffure, and the caged doves above her, symbolize the restraint and innocence of childhood. Nevertheless, Séverine is on the brink of her own first bloom, celebrated by the rapturous burst of climbing roses around the window. Profusion, strong color, and unabashed romance set the tone for the succeeding murals and rooms, which weave narrative, fact, and fable, much like life itself.

A lush blossom of 'Abraham Darby,' an English rose with a strong, fruity perfume, drops a few petals, some real and some painted. Séverine's letter, tied with satin lilac ribbon, is too faintly inscribed for the viewer to discern its message or its sender; another epistle, sealed with crimson wax, appears ready for delivery. (Opposite) A bee alights on a rose.

ROBERT

After Séverine turned seventeen, her friend Robert came often from Sault to visit her parents' cottage. When the mistral, the cold northerly wind, whistled down from Mont Ventoux, the two would sit in the kitchen talking with the cook, Céleste. On clear, warm days they strolled down lavender-bordered paths, past blazing poppies, through cypress windbreaks, on toward the oak and pine forests skirting the grand mountain. Acres of lavender spread behind them as they climbed, Robert reciting from Petrarch's love sonnets, "For Laura'll melt my soul as sun melts snow—/O hair of gold above bright sapphire eyes!" After all, Robert told Séverine, the great poet had attained the summit of Ventoux in 1336, possibly dreaming, during the ascent, of the Provençal maiden he coveted. As they entered the forest, Robert watched warily for traces of wild boar and pointed out a circlet of golden eagles flying lazily overhead. The couple envisioned an escape, Séverine from the lavender farm, Robert from the glassworks in town . . . perhaps to Paris.

Salon

TWO DOOR OPENINGS PASS from the foyer into the salon. An arched niche containing a mural depicting an older Séverine backs the hall mural of young Séverine in the window. The observer now looks out the window of the farmhouse instead of looking in. Seventeen-year-old Séverine steals into the lavender-bordered garden to meet her beau, Robert, in response to his most recent communiqué, still lying on the sill. Accoutrements from the past, including her silver

The sunlit salon features a painting of Séverine as a young woman strolling with her beau, Robert. A trompe l'oeil pot of ivy entwines the scrolled adage Carpe Diem, *or "seize the day," an admonition to young and old to live each moment to the fullest.*

French Lace

THE WORD LACE derives from the Old French *las*, for string or noose, possibly from the Latin *lacere*, to entice or ensnare; indeed, what could be more inviting than the lace-curtained windows filtering sunlight through many Provençal cottages? Linen, cotton, and silk lace evolved from early precedents, such as Egyptian openwork textiles; Anglo-Saxon drawn work and embroidery; and silver, gold, and silk netting from the Arabs and Italians. The two most common forms of handmade lace are needlepoint lace, sewn with a needle and thread, and bobbin lace, woven with bobbins around pins placed on a pillow. By the sixteenth century, Le Puy, in Auvergne, became the most important center in France for making black, white, and blond laces. In the seventeenth century, peasant women of Provence adorned cotton lawn caps, aprons, fichus or neckerchiefs, camisoles, sleeves, and shawls with generous froths of lace. Crocheted, tatting, and machine lace gained precedence over finer handmade types of lace by the early twentieth century.

comb, a satin ribbon, and a pocket watch, are left behind. Séverine's tawny hair flows freely down her back, and under her parasol she strolls in a fine citron-yellow silk skirt, occasionally glancing back to see if her parents have noticed her departure.

This mural, with the casement window thrown open and the pot of ivy seemingly set on the ledge, shows the artists' particular skill with perspective. The painters' methodology with each mural is fastidious and specific; first, they examine and measure the site where the mural is to be located, discussing with their client or designer what is required. They pay special attention to integrating the mural and the architecture in order to

A trio of unusual white French majolica asparagus plates and an English transferware platter border a window hung with panels of tambour lace. Not technically a true lace, tambour was an embroidered pattern hooked on machine-made netting beginning in the 1840s. These examples of tambour are possibly Irish.

make the trompe l'oeil effects appear more real. They give equal care to the selection of colors, which must relate to the interior decorative palette. In this instance, I supplied the artists with photographs of my daughter Rachel, who served as the model for Séverine, and with a rough sketch of the design, which they then refined. Often, the artists use references, samples of cloth, actual flowers, even antiques, to finalize the details in their drawings and paintings. Laura describes their initial drawing as a "blueprint" for the mural. They execute the drawing with graphite pencil on tracing paper using a scale of 1½" to 1.' They photocopy this pencil tracing, then they fill in the copy with colored pencils. The final presentation, or maquette, is mounted on board for the client's review. If approved, it is used as a guide for the mural. The artists transfer the design to the wall freehand and by eye only, not by a grid or projection system.

To prepare the mural surface for painting, they mix a light-colored latex house paint with acrylics. This quick-drying paint is sponged or brushed on to

An eighteenth-century French hunting scene (opposite), painted in a monochromatic style termed grisaille, *was originally set within a* boiserie, *or paneled room. The mantel (above) is all faux painted; the stone inset with a frieze of shards is called* piquer assiette, *or "stolen from plate."*

French Tiles

CERAMIC TILE production took hold in France from the end of the twelfth century as Gothic architecture inspired more elaborate decoration on the floors and walls of grand churches and residences. Eventually, towns offered subsidies to more humble homeowners for roof tiles, bricks, and floor pavers that were touted as fire preventives. Somber lead-glazed medieval tiles gave way to brightly colored tin-glazed tiles at the beginning of the sixteenth century, when Italian émigré potters introduced maiolica techniques to France. In Provence, terra-cotta tiles, both glazed and unglazed, were employed for roofs and for floors; earthen floor pavers varied in shape and size, with the small, distinctive, dry-laid hexagons known as *tomettes* appearing in the eighteenth century. Marble and patterned floor tiles were more unusual, while decorative glazed tiles were commonly used to accent fireplace surrounds and kitchen walls.

block in large areas and to create a base for an over-drawing in umber oil paint. Typically, the artists finish paintings in slow-drying oils, which allow more time for rendering detail and depth. Areas that demand fast drying or a tough finish are sometimes painted in acrylic instead. Most of the murals were not sealed or overglazed, because we wished to preserve the exact color and surface.

Remarkably, Laura and Barb paint each mural side by side. The painting is seamlessly produced with no discernible divergence between the two artists in style or execution. Most murals in the illustrated cottage took approximately a week to a month to paint, with the full decoration achieved over a three-year period.

An Old Paris porcelain teapot and creamer, their shapes inspired by the helmet forms of medieval armor, keep company on the mantel with a Staffordshire gardener. (Overleaf) A pair of Louis XIV-style carved walnut armchairs give the salon a quintessential French flavor.

An elegant arrangement (above),
including pale-peach French tulips,
lilies, and orchids by designer
Kent Choiniere, graces an English mahogany
Hepplewhite bowfront chest with ivory
escutcheons and ebony and beech string inlay.
An Old Paris tureen (left) cradles dried
ivory roses. Robert (opposite) has invited
Séverine to meet him in the garden.

MAURICE

When Séverine's parents moved to the tiny village of Sault from Paris in 1918, they brought Maurice with them. Although he had managed the gardens of the family's estate on the outskirts of Paris, the lavender farm in Sault was a new challenge for Maurice, and a hopeful venture for a family eager to improve their fortunes after the devastation of war. A rising demand from national apothecaries for healthful and beautifying products made from essential oils of lavender spurred a prosperous new industry in and around the environs of Sault. Maurice spearheaded the clearing and burning of many acres of land around the farm, and he supervised the planting of fields of *Lavandula angustifolia*, or narrow-leaf lavender, on the dry, calcareous slopes to the southwest of Mont Ventoux. The old man designed new copper stills for distilling the lavender and worked with the local farmers to create a lavender hybrid with greater yields of essential oils. In time, the land was enrobed with intense blue-mauve rows as far as the eye could see.

THE
Dining Room

BLESSED WITH BONHOMIE
and a gusto for the good life, Maurice, the old care-
taker of the lavender estate, offers a toast in the dining
room mural. He is largely responsible for the success
of the farm and for the continued good fortunes
of Séverine and Ariane's parents, whose presence is
implied although they are not actually pictured.
Indeed, Maurice and his merry wife, Céleste, have the
salubrious effect of being surrogate grandparents to
the children. Maurice is a teacher more than willing
to share his knowledge, and although humble, he is
not without sophistication, as his appreciation for a
good vintage and *Le Monde* imply.

The artists' mastery of texture is evident in
the bushiness of Maurice's brows and moustache,
in the knit of his vest, the velvety geranium leaves,
the rough-cut stone wall, and the sleek coats of the

*B*eneath a canopy of grapevines, Maurice
raises his glass (opposite) to celebrate
the results of his labors in the lavender
fields. The gardener takes his rest in the company of his beloved basset hound and tabby
cat. The family dog in real life, Betsy (above),
served as the model for Maurice's companion.

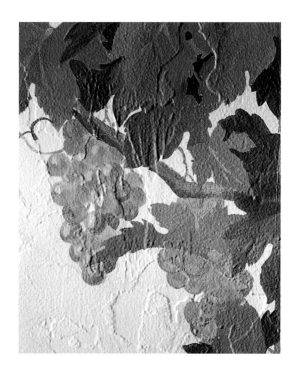

U nder the grapes (above), a faux-painted table (right) sets the stage for a simple repast with antique plates and French enamel pots à provisions. The 1920s French chandelier with white porcelain roses is a romantic cottage adaptation of grander eighteenth-century Italian fixtures. Also served with a twist—the whimsical turn-of-the-century Baroque Revival chairs. On the back wall, lavender fills a pair of rare Provençal pottery wall pockets.

hound and cat. The fields of lavender falling away in the distance are beautifully framed by the painted wooden arbor heavy with moist, plump grapes.

Maurice also drinks to another theme threading through the cottage—the cottage is really a castle, and the decoration throughout tells why. The evolution of decorative objects depends on valued materials at hand, the passion for what is fashionable, and on classic design, which eventually transcends both its period and its material. By the nineteenth century and into the twentieth, with the rise of the European bourgeoisie, cottages became miniature versions of their grander coun-

A mid-nineteenth-century New York State cupboard holds a gathering of Continental dessert plates, ironstone tureens, a tiny Staffordshire spaniel, Christmas ornaments, and majolica made by potter Andy Martin. The gilded glass pieces are nineteenth-century souvenirs found at various state fairs. A swag of bay, rosemary, sage, lavender, and crocosmia pods adorns the door.

French Breads

BREADS IN FRANCE come in a multitude of shapes and sizes, such as the irresistible, crunchy long loaf, the *baguette*, and the classic round *campagne*. In nineteenth- and early-twentieth-century Provence, breads such as the *gibassier*, a sweet bread made with orange zest and olive oil, were commonly baked on the hearth or in communal village ovens. The name *gibassier* comes from the Provençal word *gibo*, for "bump," a reference to the raised texture made by slashes across the surface. Another type of bread, the *fougasse*, has an oblong flat form incorporating a savory filling such as olives, *herbes de Provence*, and sun-dried tomatoes. In addition, there are many variations on the sweet and savory theme, such as *galettes*, or pancakes, and tarts such as the popular onion and anchovy *pissaladière*. Garlic, nuts, cheeses, and a wide variety of other ingredients, spices, and flours make breaking bread a fascinating experience.

Vineyards

T H E S T O N Y, dry soil and hot sun
of Provence nurture grapes for a dizzying
array of wines. Vineyards are concen-
trated on the rock-strewn hillsides or *côtes*
of southwestern Provence, particularly
along the southern banks of the Rhône.
Inland, for example, Châteauneuf-du-Pape,
in the Vaucluse, produces especially fine,
robust red wines. Here, large oval alluvial
stones, or *galets*, line the rows between
the vines, radiating heat during long
summer nights and helping the grapes to
attain an intense flavor and high sugar
content. Along the coast, delicious
rosés and cool reds from Bandol and dry
white wines from Cassis enhance the
sensuous flavors of garlic- and saffron-
spiced seafood. Many villages celebrate the
harvest, or *vendange*, with joyous festivals.

terparts, with the aspiring inhabitants collecting
cheaper interpretations of more costly items. In
a trompe l'oeil of their own, tole or painted tin
trays emulated expensive lacquered papier-mâché;
early lithography made tole biscuit tins and banks
in fanciful shapes very collectible—once modest in
value, they are now prized. Staffordshire mantel
ornaments and majolica potteries became the poor

man's porcelains, as did simple kitchen enamelware; painted furniture was a clever disguise of
plainer woods and primitive joinery. All developed
a certain chic and cachet if they survived to become
vintage or antique themselves. The veneration of
such wares and their particular vocabulary of style
invests the atmosphere of the cottage with another
element of "fool the eye."

*French enamel canisters (opposite) convert
to hold romantic bouquets of tuberoses,
tulips, veronica, and phlox. Below the
chandelier (left), is an early-twentieth-century
tall case clock with a Delft plate face fash-
ioned by a crockery factory worker in
New Hampshire. A tambour lace piano scarf
(above) lives a second life as a curtain.*

ÉLESTE

A purveyor *par excellence*, the keeper of the kitchen, Céleste reaped her culinary ingredients from the land outside her door. Of stalwart country stock, with gleaming white hair and teeth, Céleste arrived to cook at the farm just after the war, when the first lavender fields were planted. While her husband, Maurice, tended to the gardens, Céleste held court over the open hearth. Suckling pig, hare, rabbit, lamb, and braces of thrush and woodcock grilled over a grapevine fire, or simmered in stews rich with garlic cloves. Bundles of fennel, thyme, savory, and sage perfumed the pantry. She organized hunts for wild asparagus, morels, and snails, and she collected stores of olive oil and sheep and goat cheeses. Melons, peppers, broad beans, artichokes, and chard grew in the potager. Fig jam, almond honey, and pears poached in red wine sweetened each meal. Every week, Céleste prepared a fresh tincture of rosemary to keep the young ladies' complexions clear. Her deep laugh and her capacious bosom embraced the sisters Séverine and Ariane, and their cousin Delphine.

THE Kitchen

THE CONCEPT OF CÉLESTE was truly the catalyst for both the decorating scheme and the Provençal fable. When I first arrived at the cottage, the rooms were dark, the tile floors a harsh terra-cotta, the maple kitchen cabinets simple but without distinction. The house felt cramped and a bit cold. Immediately, my goal was to lighten and brighten the spaces. The kitchen was the place the family gathered, and the main focal point was the hollow-core door leading out to the garage. The door had no moldings and held no promise for anything exciting behind it. Right away, I felt compelled to create a warm, ebullient presence there, a kitchen goddess clothed in Provençal colors. Hardworking, jovial, always producing delicious smells and tastes from the garden, Céleste was conceived as an archetypal earth mother.

*T*ransforming a once unattractive hollow-core door (opposite) leading from the kitchen to the garage, Céleste's convivial demeanor and harvest basket full of lavender connote her role as a provider of plenty with a cunning economy of means. The artists skillfully matched the color and perspective of the tile floor, and humorously incorporated a cat door. (Above) The French symbol of virility, the rooster.

Carrying an enormous basket of lavender, sur-rounded by clucking chickens, Céleste now brings abundant harvest into the kitchen all year long.

Barb, Laura, and I planned Céleste to com-plement other color changes in the kitchen and throughout the cottage made by housepainter and finish specialist David Schultz, particularly those on the floors. David devised an ingenious way of whitewashing the orange-brown Mexican tile, although he cautions that adequate preparations are absolutely critical, and even then the method is not foolproof, especially in very high-traffic areas

The kitchen exudes a jolly gypsy wagon spirit with its deep Chinese-red walls and turquoise-glazed cabinetry. Painter David Schultz applied the cabinet glaze with a feather duster to achieve a subtle stippled effect. Adding to the cheerful cacaphony: Sienese pot-tery, French enameled pots, and a 1920s French gilt bronze and milk-glass chandelier. An antiques dealer friend jokes that the refrigera-tor is a contemporary form of enamelware.

or in areas exposed to constant moisture. Also, another tile with a different finish will certainly react otherwise to this method and materials. Most of the materials he suggests are available at paint stores. First, we very thoroughly scrubbed the floor clean with TSP (trisodium phosphate) solution. David then rinsed and dried the floor at least three times (any TSP left would shed the new finish). A dull surface remained, which was further rubbed down with synthetic abrasives such as Scotch-Brite. The floor was then vacuumed and rubbed with a tack cloth to pick up any remaining particles of dust. Working in sections, David brushed a light,

A comparison of postcards featuring the work of French and Italian painters and the palette suffusing the kitchen proves a Mediterranean influence. Stacked next to an enormous 1920s brass Indian tray, Sienese chargers are gaily hand-painted with the crests or contrades *of the seventeen families who compete twice yearly in the famous horse race, the Palio.*

Enamelware

ENAMELING IS an ancient technique of applying a paste of powdered glass and colored metallic oxide to a metal base such as copper or tin, and fusing it to the base by a heating process. In sixteenth-century France, Limoges enamels popularized the process, and as the application became less expensive, enamelware became the poor man's porcelain. Humbler objects such as snuffboxes and candlesticks were produced, and, by the early twentieth century, lots of kitchenware. Graduated canisters, or *séries des pots*, for dry goods such as sugar, flour, coffee, and tea; coffeepots (*cafetières*); milk pitchers (*pots à lait*); soap dishes (*porte-savons*); salt boxes (*boîtes à sel*); ladles with racks (*porte-louches*); and match holders (*boîtes à allumettes*) are classics now avidly collected at French flea markets.

An amusing juxtaposition of real and painted Sienese platters (above) reveals the fate of airborne crockery. Voluptuous pillows (opposite), including a dusty-pink vintage Fortuny, lend the cottage a bit of splendor, as does the 1930s French chinoiserie chandelier.

even coat of Benjamin Moore's oil-base Pickling White on the floor, which was then pounced with rags and sponges to achieve an aged, slightly mottled effect. He defined and emphasized the grout lines by wiping out an additional bit of finish with a foam brush. This stage was left to dry for three days. Finally, he applied three coats of Benjamin Moore Stays Clear acrylic polyurethane in a low-luster sheen, rubbing with Scotch-Brite, vacuuming, and cleaning with a tack cloth between each coat. Spot touch-ups are needed about every three years. Very labor-intensive, but the light tile floors, in tandem with pickled wooden floors, effected a remarkable transformation in the small cottage, making it seem twice as large. Laura and Barb then did a marvelous job of continuing the perspective of the tile floors within their trompe l'oeil door, so that it appears that Céleste is entering the kitchen from a similarly tiled courtyard.

Another tile problem was posed by the existing kitchen counter backsplash and stove hood. I was not fond of the tile, but rather than blasting it

Provençal Cuisine

LAMB GRILLED with branches of rosemary; *tapenade*, a spread for toast or raw vegetables blended with tuna, anchovies, mustard, cognac, and capers; luscious *aïoli*, a mayonnaise unguent with olive oil, egg yolk, and garlic—Provençal food is not for those with shy palates. Savory, aromatic, satisfying, especially when washed down with a few glasses of wine, local cooking reflects the ingredients available fresh daily. Along the coast, fish such as rascasse, John Dory, monkfish, conger eel, and cod star in fish soup or *bouillabaisse*. Saffron, almonds, cinnamon, currants, and orange peel lend an Arab piquancy to stews such as beef *daube*. Spinach, chard, tomato, basil, and cheese bubble in rich vegetable *gratins*, while fresh black truffle grated into scrambled eggs, *brouillade*, is a particular favorite.

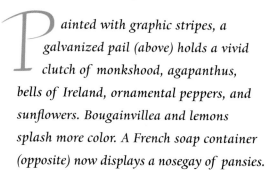

Painted with graphic stripes, a galvanized pail (above) holds a vivid clutch of monkshood, agapanthus, bells of Ireland, ornamental peppers, and sunflowers. Bougainvillea and lemons splash more color. A French soap container (opposite) now displays a nosegay of pansies.

all out, I decided to tame it by juxtaposing very strong jolts of complementary colors. My daughter Ana chose a deep red for the walls, and David Schultz created a lovely turquoise for the cabinets, using an oil-base satin-finish underpaint, then, with a feather duster, stippling on a slightly muddied, transparent teal oil-base overglaze.

Garlic Rabbit
Lapin à l'Ail

SERVES 4

Large pinch of coarse sea salt
Pepper
3 garlic cloves, peeled
Large pinch of crumbled
        thyme leaves
3 tablespoons olive oil
1 rabbit, cut up as for a sauté
¼ cup white wine

Preheat the oven to 375°F. In a mortar, pound the salt, pepper, and garlic to a paste with a wooden pestle. Stir in the thyme and olive oil. Put the rabbit pieces in a large bowl, spoon over the garlic mixture, and rub all the rabbit pieces in your hands to thoroughly coat them. Arrange them side by side in a shallow baking dish and put it in the oven. After 20 minutes, turn the pieces over, bring the white wine to a boil, add it to the baking dish, and baste two or three times during the next 20 minutes. Bake for about 40 minutes in all, or until the thigh is tender when pierced with a trussing needle.

DELPHINE

During the high summer, the sisters would invite their French-American cousin, Delphine, to the farm for several weeks. The cousins awoke each morning, drank their tisanes, and as the trickling dew dried on the roses, they played pell-mell through the lavender-scented *mas*, the carriage house, the potager, the fields, even the vineyards near the Nesques gorges. Delphine was Séverine's age—she loved to tease Séverine about Robert. Above all, she loved to set up an easel and paint the lavender fields backlit by the sun. Old Maurice sold his more camphorous *Lavandula latifolia* to a dealer in Sault for the manufacture of paints and varnishes—he managed to procure some of the dealer's pigments for the avid Delphine, who showed precocious talent for depicting the landscapes around the farm. Broad slashes of lapis, mauve, ochre, vermilion, olive, and russet thrust across her canvases. Her visions were born again years later, in 1936, when as a bohemian artist with Proustian wistfulness and a passion for the botanical, Delphine painted her memories on the walls of a diminutive cottage in America.

T H E
Atelier

WITH PROVENCE'S LONG tradition of being home to countless artists, it is only fitting that the studio of the cottage belongs to Delphine, my artistic alter ego and free spirit. The atelier, once a stark white room, now features two contiguous walls painted—in my imagination by Delphine—with vistas of lavender fields from the farm in Sault. The challenge was to capture the luminous colors of a landscape in Provence and to integrate the mural almost seamlessly into the room itself. This mural is painted more impressionistically than the others, and the vantage point is aerial—indeed, the onlooker might be a bird winging through the atelier. For speed and ease, base colors of melon, ochre, green, and buff were sponged on with latex house paint, then further details, including rows of lavender and sunflowers, were sponged and brushed on with latex house paint mixed with acrylics. The artists did a master-

*A*rtist's tools of the trade (opposite) set the tone for Delphine's studio against a still life by Laura Chappell. An Eastlake bookcase (above) supports a collection of antique French and American Indian baskets. The marble-topped maple table was once used for making pastries.

rench doors (left) shed light on a glorious Provençal landscape, the scene of the lavender farm from Delphine's childhood sojourns in Sault. A new chandelier made with bits and pieces of old ones, and festooned with violet and scarlet drops, continues the theme of tongue-in-cheek glitter. Herb candles (above) await evening.

ful job of creating subtle gradations in tone, a limpid atmosphere, and a sense of broad expanse.

A 1934 Parisian floral still life with jewel-like colors, above the fireplace, also guided the decorative palette. Then, to match the daring of the mural, the room is dressed as if it is in costume. Cotton toile and silk plaid curtains are thrown up on iron rods as if they were remnants of frivolous ball gowns put to more practical use. Continuing the fancy dress theme are voluptuous pillows and a medley of layered upholstery fabrics and rugs. A nineteenth-century French rosewood gent's arm-chair and a walnut English side chair are covered in

Painted an exceptional shade of mauve, a lift-top chest from the Czech Republic was made to look more like an elegant commode by designing two faux drawers above a real one to conceal the blanket box. A green tole container houses an armful of dried larkspur to blend with the painted fields of lavender above, while Chanticleer reviews a gathering of French pottery.

Lavender

POSSESSING THE most characteristic color and scent of Provence, lavender is a shrubby, aromatic herb related to the mint family, along with its cousins rosemary, sage, and thyme. Native to the Mediterranean, the plant grew wild in southern France or was natu-ralized there by the Phocaeans. Provençal peasants valued lavender for its healing, antiseptic, and calming properties, using its essential oils to salve wounds and repel insects. Fresh or dried flowers were strewn on floors and linens and used in cooking; its oils infused medicinal preparations, soaps, and perfumes. Lavender was gathered wild until the end of the nineteenth cen-tury; the beginning of the twentieth marked the advent of commercial fields. Three types are grown. The original wild *Lavandula angustifolia*, or narrow-leaf lavender, grows best at higher altitudes and yields the finest essential oil. *Lavandula latifolia*, or broad-leaf, is more camphoric and grows at moderate altitudes. Since the 1920s, a hybrid of the two, lavandin, or *Lavandula X intermedia*, has been planted heavily. The yields of essential oils are less fine but much greater.

Designer Kent Choiniere used antique glazed French earthenware jars filled with floral foam to secure mounds of hydrangeas (above) and zinnias, delphinium, monkshood, and greenish-yellow bupleurum (opposite). Mexican glass balls mirror the flowers.

velvety boarskin suede. Buff canvas slipcovers drape a chaise and settee, which are given an illusion of motion by the rugs and a low, central table set on angles. A primitive, green-painted potting table found in a Colorado barn, now used as a sideboard, coexists fashionably with a pair of formal French Empire mahogany commodes. In keeping with the "castle in a cottage" motif, the mantel is "faux"; the transverse piece was salvaged from an old garage, then supported on two corbels to give the brick chimney breast more presence. Once dull red, the bricks were softly whitewashed to blend more successfully with other elements in the room.

The history of French fabrics influenced my textile choices for the atelier. *Les indiennes,* seventeenth-century hand-printed French cotton fabrics copied from Indian examples, evolved into stunning copperplate and roller-printed cottons, or *toiles de Jouy,* at the famous Oberkampf factories at Jouy-en-Josas at the end of the eighteenth century. At one point, thousands of mulberry trees grew in Provence to feed the worms for a booming silk

Artistic Traditions

THE CLARITY of light and the brilliant colors revealed by the light diffused over the Provençal landscape have attracted an extraordinary assemblage of artists, including painters, writers, craftsmen, and artisans of every stripe. Some of the great names associated with Provence: Pierre Bonnard, Albert Camus, Paul Cézanne, Marc Chagall, Coco Chanel, Jean Cocteau, Colette, André Derain, Raoul Dufy, Lawrence Durrell, F. Scott Fitzgerald, Paul Gauguin, Jean Giono, Ernest Hemingway, D. H. Lawrence, Fernand Léger, Katherine Mansfield, Henri Matisse, W. Somerset Maugham, Frédéric Mistral, Anaïs Nin, Nostradamus, Marcel Pagnol, Francesco Petrarch, Pablo Picasso, Pierre-Auguste Renoir, Edmond Rostand, Antoine de Saint-Exupéry, Madame de Sévigné, Gertrude Stein, Vincent Van Gogh.

Holding a pannier of sweet peas, the imagined figure of Delphine (opposite) affects a gypsy-like mien in a 1920 canvas by French artist André Brunin. The well-used palette (above) is witness to Delphine's prolific painting. (Overleaf) A collection of still lifes, framed and unframed, amplifies the botanical themes of the atelier.

A 1930s Bessarabian kilim (above), a tapestry-woven rug, is striking for its tribal interpretation of a floral design. French toile and silk plaid (right) cover down-filled pillows embellished with pretty trims. Adding to the "gypsy tent" effect, curtains (opposite) billow with silk plaid, toile, and unsewn panels with portraits of nomadic peoples.

industry. Provençal designers created distinctive silk and cotton *boutis,* or bed covers, quilted with images of pomegranates, melons, hearts, and other symbols of fertility. Plants and insects yielded natural dyes with brilliant colors: woad and indigo for rich blues; madder root, the eggs of the parasitic insect—the kermes—and its relative, cochineal, for reds; and sumac stalks, woadwaxen root, and buck-

thorn fruit for yellows. The stalks of the fustic plant made an orange-yellow much favored in Provence called, translated from the Provençal language, the color of a kiss to my beloved.

It is this intense riot of texture and hue, a madness with method, that I attempted to translate to the atelier, and it signifies Delphine's willingness to take calculated risks, artistically and otherwise.

Textiles

THE EVOLUTION of French fabrics, particularly printed cloth, is rooted in the traditional textiles of India, where artisans perfected ancient methods of dyeing with mordants and wax resists to make colorfast fabrics. By 1664, the Campagnie des Indes-Orientales imported bales of exotic hand-blocked printed cottons, called *calicots* or *chints* from India to Marseille. The vibrantly hued, intricate patterns, known more broadly as *les indiennes*, became the rage for costumes and furnishings. Colorfast paisleys, geometrics, and botanical, animal, and mythic themes abounded in brilliant shades of saffron, vermilion, indigo, bronze, honey, olive, and russet. In the mid-seventeenth century, Marseille playing-card manufacturers first attempted to cut woodblocks for printing cotton cloth. Numerous ateliers devoted to copying *les indiennes* sprang up, but not until 1734 did the French fully understand the Indian process of mordants, key to making textiles colorfast.

 I Ñ A

Sixty years after Delphine painted the scenes of her childhood sojourns in Sault, the illustrated cottage came up for sale. A woman intent on creating a new life came to see the property at twilight. She saw a squirrel finial atop a quizzical three-peaked shingled roof. A neglected dooryard garden enclosed by a latticed wooden fence stood lonely and overgrown. Even the dovecote against the chimney looked abandoned. Old French verdigris copper lanterns shed a dim glow on the cottage. When the woman stepped inside, she saw the famous paintings, the Provençal lavender fields, the characters in Delphine's story. She understood the message of the little cottage at once: the importance of dreams, of beauty, of the artist's penchant for light and color. Delphine's raison d'être was her own. Her drive to make visions from the mind's eye real for others made her Delphine's legacy. The woman bought the cottage, made a nest for her two beautiful daughters, and commenced planting a garden. She saw with her heart that a new life and a new love were hers.

THE
Boudoir

IN MY MIND, AND IN THE fairy tale, the stairway to the upstairs bedroom bridges the transition from Delphine's 1936 cottage to my own life. It represents the visual and philosophical leap from the past to the present, and the passing of the stewardship of the illustrated cottage from Delphine to myself.

The ascent is marked by painted bits and pieces of life's vanities dropped along the steps—some loose stems of lavender and roses, a linen handkerchief marked with the initial "N," a broken strand of pearls, a compact of lip rouge (my most adored accessory), and a pair of opulent embroidered slippers. Through this wake of feminine appurtenances scurries a tiny mouse. Eager to escape the three family cats, just as I am often eager to retreat from life's storms, the mouse makes for

*B*etsy the basset hound (above) ambles down the stairs painted with faux "runners." Painter David Schultz first taped off the design, then executed the runners in high-gloss oil-base enamel paint. The artists later applied details such as the handkerchief (opposite).

With regal dignity, Sneakers the senior feline (left) reposes at the foot of a late-nineteenth-century French bed of pickled beech delicately carved with roses. English transferware and American spongeware trace the arc of the headboard. A 1920s French crystal chandelier (above) evokes grandeur in the garret.

Clues to the penchants of the lady of the house are strewn along the steps (above): a broken strand of luminous pearls and a silver compact of rouge. A mouse, painted after the artists spied the cat bringing one inside, tracks through the rouge to safety. A pair of slippers (right) appears to have been left behind.

safety above. Apparently the term boudoir, which includes a woman's private bedroom, dressing, and sitting areas, derives from the Old French word *bouder*, which means to sulk or to pout. Having discovered that pouting feels far more solitary than constructive thinking, I prefer to use my own boudoir for positive rest and reflection. In fact, the little office off my bedroom provided the sanctuary for designing and writing *The Illustrated Cottage*. The office holds several bookcases stuffed with gardening and decorating books, and visual cues for design projects are strewn everywhere; scraps of fabrics, paint chips, framed collections of butterfly wings for color inspiration, catalogs, and the curse of editors and writers everywhere—precarious piles of papers. At the top of the stairwell, a lacy bra appears to be flung casually over the ledge. Another example of the artists' remarkable trompe l'oeil painting, the bra makes an important feminist statement. Although I embrace all things pretty and feminine, and I love being a woman, I shall cast off such frivolities to maintain freedom! Delphine's maverick ways are a true reflection of my own.

In the relative peace of the boudoir, my daughter Rachel helped me to develop the character of her counterpart, lovely Séverine, and, a fine creative writer, she gave me cogent advice on editing this book. Friends such as antiques dealer Janice Woods arrived from time to time to check on my

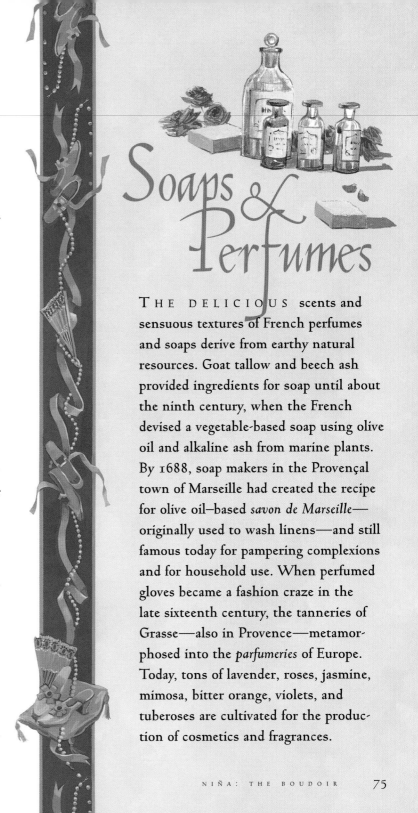

Soaps & Perfumes

THE DELICIOUS scents and sensuous textures of French perfumes and soaps derive from earthy natural resources. Goat tallow and beech ash provided ingredients for soap until about the ninth century, when the French devised a vegetable-based soap using olive oil and alkaline ash from marine plants. By 1688, soap makers in the Provençal town of Marseille had created the recipe for olive oil–based *savon de Marseille*— originally used to wash linens—and still famous today for pampering complexions and for household use. When perfumed gloves became a fashion craze in the late sixteenth century, the tanneries of Grasse—also in Provence—metamorphosed into the *parfumeries* of Europe. Today, tons of lavender, roses, jasmine, mimosa, bitter orange, violets, and tuberoses are cultivated for the production of cosmetics and fragrances.

progress. Known for her great eye and good-hearted wit, Janice was constantly on the lookout for antiques that would fit with the French artist and gypsy themes. In keeping with these themes, broken platters, tiles, and mosaics appear throughout the cottage, symbolic of the colorful bits and pieces of Delphine's memories. Janice reveled in finding items such as a Victorian planter embedded with many charming fragments of tiles and plates, an example of a folk art technique sometimes called memory-ware. Another design maven, Lyn Martin, a brilliant practitioner of the "more is more" school of decorating, was extremely adept at finding old tole trays and porcelain platters. Laura Chappell donated her French-American grandmother's name, Delphine, to the artist of the fairy tale. Her grandmother had been a painter, skillful at executing beautiful oil floral still lifes. Shopkeeper Jean Snow brought over tiny nests, eggs, and a collection of milliner's feathers in extraordinary, deep colors. On vacations, Ana and Rachel gathered armfuls of exquisite seashells on Bahamian beaches and pottery shards along the

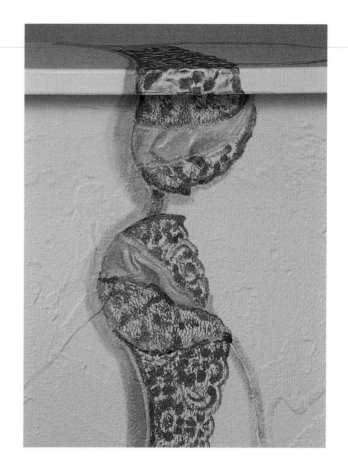

*I*n the stairwell of the dressing area *(opposite), hangs another 1920s French chandelier. A gilded English Regency mirror with a string-of-pearl-beaded frame recalls the owner's propensity for pearls, while the brassiere (above) reveals a wish for both beauty and emancipation.*

Crystal Chandeliers

THE INVENTION of lead crystal in about 1676 by George Ravenscroft in England served as the chief catalyst in the development of glass chandeliers. Attempting to alleviate some technical problems in the making of glass, Ravenscroft added red lead, creating a heavy, brilliantly clear, sonorous, white glass. The glass was dense, refractive, and easily engraved and faceted—characteristics that made crystal well suited for the cutting of elaborate chandeliers, lanterns, candelabra, goblets, optical lenses, and glass for watch faces. Glass chandeliers were first designed early in the eighteenth century in England and Italy. In France, the Royal Glassworks of Saint Louis duplicated the same quality of lead crystal by 1781, and the French firms Saint Louis and Baccarat became celebrated for their magnificent crystal chandeliers.

coast of Italy to fill bowls back home. Francophile Katherine Whitcomb, who haunted the same antiques shops I did, would return with tales of copper French lanterns, or some other vital necessity for the cottage. Magazine colleagues such as editor Rachel Newman and photographer Keith Scott Morton, both quite accustomed to humoring my vagaries in style over the years, never accused me once of obsession. Indeed, I relied on untold numbers of family members and friends to help me develop the wild alchemy to its fullest extent. It is wonderful how many were happy to comply, perhaps an indication of the importance of fantasy in all of our lives.

Testament to fragility, a shattered English transferware platter accompanies a watercolor sketch, antique Delft tiles, a silver cup of mauve 'Angel Face' roses, and two oils of roses. The larger canvas was painted by the French artist Marthe Orant, allegedly Édouard Vuillard's mistress.

RIANE

The younger sister, Ariane, felt most comfortable with the animals on the farm, and her favored domain was the carriage house, where many of the beasts lived. In late summer, Céleste would send Ariane to pick bunches of lavender to dry inside the linen armoire. Ariane, often brash and adventurous as long as her black dog, Biscuit, accompanied her, spent hours in the fields picking wild strawberries and investigating badger holes. Her original errand finally completed, Ariane would stop to inspect her litter of young lop rabbits and to feed a few apples to the livestock. Both Biscuit and the pig excelled at truffle hunting, with the pig perhaps winning the contest. The pig lorded her status over the gentle Camargue horse, saved from herding bulls when Ariane's father bid on him, then a colt, during a trip to the coast. It was the child's greatest pleasure to ride her horse bareback in the afternoon, sometimes with her older cousin Delphine behind her. The smell of the *garrigue*, scrub full of wild thyme, pervaded their dusty trail while the cicadas sang crisply in the late light.

T H E
Carriage House

THE RENOVATION OF A FOR-
merly dark, dank garage into a functional living
space, the carriage house, was possibly the most
dramatic transformation in the cottage. The seed
of the idea was planted by antiques dealer Eron
Johnson, who observed that quarters were a bit
cramped for two children, three dogs, three cats,
and numerous antiques, and needed expanding. At
first I demurred, having taken on quite a bit already
with the decoration of the original house. The
more I thought about it, however, the more I saw
that Eron was right; the twenty-two-foot-square
garage, directly attached to the house off the
kitchen, was double height with a makeshift loft.
Here was an opportunity to afford the family a
great deal more room and to create a dramatic,
soaring space that would flood more light into the

*A posterior view of Céleste (above) is
painted on the back of the door leading
from the kitchen into the carriage
house. Formerly a garage, the carriage
house (opposite) is decorated with a collection of photographs and eighteenth-century
French engravings of farm animals.*

Heavy 1920s wrought-iron settee and armchairs (right) once withstood more exposure on a verandah. The doors, salvaged from an old building, were refitted to replace an overhead garage door. Repeating the iron motif, a wrought-iron and sheet metal stove (above) coexists with an eighteenth-century English candle lantern.

Painted to resemble a stable interior, a bank of cabinets (opposite) conceals the television, stereo system, and additional storage. Although the mural measures 11'8" by 8'3", the artists drew the entire composition without the aid of a grid system. Pots (above) stack behind doors.

cottage—while increasing the total square footage of the house from approximately 2,400 to 3,000 square feet. With somewhat the same sensation that one experiences when leaping off a cliff, I called on contractor Marcel Doyon to help me design, engineer, and build the room as well as a new garage. Marcel and I had worked on several projects together, and I had confidence that he could interpret my plan successfully.

I found the concept of a rustic but light-filled barn very appealing, and I wanted to retain some hint of the room's original purpose while integrating it within the Provençal fairy tale. Thus the vision of a carriage house on the lavender estate used to house farm equipment, vehicles, and domestic animals was born. While Marcel and his assistant, Al Johnson, commenced demolition within the garage, I began deliberations with Laura and Barb on the design for another mural.

This time, I wished to use my younger daughter, Ana, as the model for her French counterpart, animal-loving Ariane. Enamored of four-footed

Livestock

FOR CENTURIES, Provençal country folk maintained intimate connections with their farm animals; sheep actually functioned as warmers under certain types of shepherd beds. Oxen and donkeys pulled plows, while goats foraging on the herb-strewn moor provided rich cheeses such as *banon*, wrapped in chestnut leaves. Succulent lamb, kid, and rabbit were raised as traditional favorites for stews called *daubes*. Many farmsteads, dependent on egg money, kept flocks of pigeons in dovecotes called *pigeonniers*, as well as chickens, geese, guinea fowl, and Muscovy ducks. From the eighteenth century, even silkworms were raised and nurtured on mulberry leaves in special attics called *magnaneries*. Prized pigs, especially in the Vaucluse, hunted truffles alongside farm dogs or became spicy sausage. Southwest, in the marshy Camargue, the *gardians* bred an ancient strain of white horses to herd the local black bulls.

creatures from early childhood, Ana manifested the proper karma for inhabiting the Provençal barn. As before, I supplied references, photographs, and a sketch, laying out very carefully the disposition of Ariane, the barn animals, and the architectural elements to portray in the mural. Again, it was critical to mesh the trompe l'oeil elements with the actual structure of the room. We discussed the project in detail with Marcel and painter David Schultz in order to ensure that the new construction and other painted finishes would blend with the mural. While the artists refined the maquette, or drawing, for the mural, I continued working with Marcel.

We were so accustomed to working together that, with engineering specifications, we were able to proceed without any detailed architectural plans. Often this happy collaboration is not feasible, and

A raucana chicken eggs (opposite) inspired subtle colors in the mural where Ariane's Camargue horse (left) greets the portly but friendly truffle-hunting pig. The artist Barb Fisher's handling of the steed's docile face and stance is particularly sensitive. A curious mouse (above) peeks bright-eyed from the tool bin.

even with projects that appear very simple, home-owners are advised to be cautious—not the least to protect themselves from their own errors. I made several during the course of the project, but with Marcel's guidance, we were able to avert problems before final construction. The garage wall and ceiling studs were insulated and braced in preparation for dry walling. We designed some simple pine box beams to emphasize the vault of the ceiling and

A painted nineteenth-century Normandy buffet à deux corps (opposite and right) holds plates made by potter Joyce Pashel. Similar cupboards with fruit and flower carvings signifying fertility were often given as marriage gifts in the French provinces. A lime-washed jar (above) stored olive oil or pickling brine.

A nineteenth-century French Baroque
Revival wrought-iron chandelier (above)
is suspended dramatically from the
twenty-foot ceiling. A cast bronze and wool
ram by artist Charles Kurtz stands sentinel
by the settee. The ladder leads up to the loft
bed (right), draped with a hand-printed
Provençal quilt. Affixed to iron rods across
the windows, arrowhead finials originally
topped a gate to a Normandy church.

Ironwork

ACCORDING TO antiques dealer and collector Eron Johnson, the French were prolific makers of iron, and particularly from Napoleonic times forward, they used wrought and cast iron for decorative and structural elements inside buildings as much as for exteriors. The nature of iron offered stalwart security and protection while affording great decorative whimsy and creativity. Blacksmiths during the eighteenth-century Baroque and Rococo periods forged a plethora of grilles, screens, railings, balconies, stairways, columns, canopies, fanlights, hardware, lanterns, signs, fences, and gates. Eventually, iron gazebos, conservatories, awnings, and outdoor furniture transformed parks and gardens. French iron was shipped in large quantities to colonies such as the West Indies, to cities such as New Orleans, and to markets all over the world.

detailed the finials of the loft balustrade and handrails to match those made for the garden fences. A pine plank floor was laid with insulation over the original concrete floor. A frankly ugly metal garage door was carted away and replaced by a pair of old carriage house doors, found at a salvage shop and refurbished to fit. An antique window was placed to let light into the loft. The basic process, including building the new garage and

landscaping newly created sideyards and backyards, took place over eight months.

Once these tasks were completed, David Schultz moved in with his assistant Greg Fajardo to paint and glaze. The rough-plastered walls were painted creamy off-white, like the whitewash of an old French barn, and David pickled the floors to blend with the other tile and wooden floors throughout the cottage. He painted the balustrade

*U*p in the loft (above), a model of a thatched-roof stable, a French screened food safe, a Mexican lantern, and a collection of baskets continue the rustic theme. Contractor Marcel Doyon designed sawhorse legs to create a table from an old Mexican shutter. On the bedside stand (opposite), a cast-iron lamp sheds light on a piggy bank—emphasizing the importance of les cochons in Provence.

and beams with the same creamy flat latex, then rubbed and distressed surfaces with rags, rocks, ice picks, and chains, finally brushing on a gentle umber glaze. A weathered-looking crackle finish was applied to the inside of the carriage house doors. Laura and Barb then executed the mural with latex, acrylics, and oils in about a month, using more muted tones than those in the other paintings.

The exterior of the carriage house (opposite) clearly shows the refurbished salvaged doors and new patio garden. Retaining its original opalescent glass, the verdigris copper American lantern (above left) was inspired by a French Gothic design. A 1920s French wirework garden chair (above) helps set the lighthearted scene (overleaf) for impromptu drinking and dining alfresco.

FLORA

In Niña's garden flourishes a white peony she calls Flora, a plant with flowers of such luminous and nascent beauty that the most jaded and hardened soul is compelled to bury himself and all his senses within the tissuelike freshness of the blossoms. This long-lived peony is surrounded by many other flowers—sweetly fragrant crimson, mauve, and ivory roses, spikes of lavender, lemon-scented thyme, crinkled salmon poppies, apricot agastache, purple verbena, snowy narcissus, green hellebores, royal blue irises, silver artemisia, and countless other aromatic and lovely plants, all honoring the heritage of the illustrated cottage. The seductive perfume of spring hyacinths beckons passersby to the door. August hawk moths sip nectar from honey-scented buddleias. By autumn, crabapples, viburnums, and cotoneasters set scarlet fruits amid frothy asters, while hydrangeas mellow to deep buff-pink and amethyst. In winter, hardy pansies peek shyly from the stubble. Onlookers imagine wandering through the garden, up the steps into the storybook cottage.

T H E
Garden

MY LOVE OF GARDENING
is perhaps the single greatest impetus behind the
design of the illustrated cottage. When I first spot-
ted the 1936 cottage in late spring, even without
extensive gardens it exuded a quaint charm. The
architecture of the cottage was not classically
Provençal or French, but the triple-peaked wood
shingle roof gave the house a French country air. A
friend, garden designer Diane Row, and I decided

*G lowing in the late afternoon light,
hardy pansies and chrysanthemums
await planting in the September
garden. Tiered rock walls border two
extended beds around the front perimeter
of the cottage, while the fence, copied
from an eighteenth-century French design,
encloses a series of dooryard gardens.*

to plan an exuberant garden, investing the beds surrounding the cottage with Gallic flair. Although the property was not large, this was no small undertaking in the arid, alpine Zone 4 climate of Colorado.

Diane's vast knowledge of a wide range of local and exotic perennials, trees, and shrubs, coupled with her stint of horticultural training in France and England, helped impart the sophisticated yet ingenuous quality the garden required. Diane says, "I placed plants chosen for their individual beauty into a concert of rhythmic and repetitive patterns." The "bones" of the garden—the granite-walled beds, latticed fence, and pyramidal *tuteurs*, wooden structures to support vines—provided constructive geometry for plant masses undulating throughout the garden. Diane wove ribbons of planting with particular attention to color and textural harmonies. We collaborated on translating the gypsy-inspired color palette from the interior to the outside, and Diane orchestrated the most salient hues in her positioning of the shrubs and foliage anchoring the beds: golden-chartreuse

*W*inding through a ladder (above), a hop vine, with its distinctive inflorescence, seeks any vertical support. Always valuable for increasing the visual feast, many vines grow here: clematis, Virginia creeper, honeysuckle, grape, silver fleece, and hyacinth bean. Tools (opposite) stand ready to cultivate the soil.

'Goldflame' spireas, gray-blue Arctic willows, teal spruces, garnet 'Crimson Pygmy' barberries and Cistena plums, and gray-green 'Holger' junipers. From there, we mixed silver, sage, sapphire, lilac, opal, and persimmon, always considering a progression of continuous bloom and interesting structure throughout each season.

Perennial beds (opposite), anchored with dwarf spruces, junipers, spireas, willows, and barberries, are enclosed by New York State granite mortared from behind to appear dry-stacked. A carved wooden squirrel (left) on the roof, and a dovecote (above) on the chimney add cottage charm.

A fragrant dwarf crabapple (opposite) called 'Sugar Tyme' blooms in April. Its pink buds burst into snowy blossoms, then form tiny currant-red fruit. A procession of spring bulbs join the show: hyacinths, daffodils, allium, and tulips such as pink-fringed 'Fancy Frills' (above) and apricot-flushed 'Daydream' (right).

Provençal Gardens

HERB-SCENTED parterres, the drone of honeybees, and the evening song of nightingales enchant garden strollers in Provence, where plots are influenced not only by the classical symmetry of traditional French gardens but also by the terraced effect of gardens in Italy. Elegant country villas, *bastides*, feature stark open terraces along the façade, surrounded by formal borders edged in box, with kitchen gardens and orchards beyond. Houses are shaded with wisteria or grapevine-laden trellises and sheltered with fringes of pine, fig, poplar, linden, or plane trees. Massive glazed earthen pots and urns spill over with ebullient geraniums. The famous footed vases from Anduze, often planted with orange and lemon trees, are so heavy they require their own wooden cart to transport them from the greenhouse.

Larry Horgan, Gene Motnyk, Marné Harney, Alfredo Varela, and several others were stellar in building the walls, fencing, flagstone paths, and beds, and in planting and maintaining the garden. We installed French antique verdigris lanterns, a dovecote, a carved squirrel roof finial, specially turned fence finials, and a rustic French bench. The garden elicits

endless curiosity and admiration for its architectural underpinnings and unusual plant combinations.

In creating a cottage garden, sometimes art-lessness is necessary to avoid a slick quality—the soulfulness of a mistake can teach and even disarm. Here, thankfully, nature offers plenty of opportunities to learn from one's mistakes.

*M*uch appreciated in early spring for their powerfully sweet perfume and candy colors, hyacinths are planted with great abandon in the dooryard to greet visitors: mauve-pink 'Splendid Cornelia' (above), deep blue 'Peter Stuyvesant' (left), and carmine 'Jan Bos' (opposite).

*T*oby the pewter-gray cat (right) surveys activity in the garden. Beet-purple tulip 'Passionale' (above) mingles with the variegated ground cover lamium 'White Nancy,' and fragrant orange tulip 'General de Wet' (below). (Overleaf) A romantic crimson English rose, 'L. D. Braithwaite,' stands out against the dark teal-blue fence.

*A*rtemisia 'Valerie Finnis' (opposite) and
the rapidly spreading green-and-white
ground cover lamium create a striking
contrast with Triumph tulip 'Passionale.'
Also blooming in spring: the starry florets
of allium christophii (top left) and delicious
double daffodil 'Petit Four' (bottom left). In
June the roses begin, including lemon-scented
mauve floribunda 'Angel Face' (above),
notable for its open, many-petaled blossoms.

The last rays of light (right) glow amid preparations for a soirée. Approached through the arched gate from the front garden, the patio is furnished with mismatched 1920s French iron tables and chairs, pots of vibrant bougainvillea, and trompe l'oeil lemon trees. The gate to the patio (above) is surmounted by wisteria.

BIBLIOGRAPHY

Art History

Stokstad, Marilyn. *Art History*. New York: Harry N. Abrams, Inc., 1995.

Authors

Cheetham, Erika. *The Final Prophecies of Nostradamus*. New York: The Berkley Publishing Group, 1989.

Fabre, Jean-Henri. *The Passionate Observer*. San Francisco: Chronicle Books, 1998.

Fortescue, Lady Winifred. *Perfume from Provence*. Great Britain: William Blackwood & Sons Ltd., 1935; preface by Patricia Wells. New York: Hearst Books, 1993.

Mayle, Peter. *A Year in Provence*. Great Britain: Hamish Hamilton, Ltd., 1989; New York: Alfred A. Knopf, 1997.

———. *Toujours Provence*. Great Britain: Hamish Hamilton, Ltd., 1991; New York: Alfred A. Knopf, 1991.

The Memoirs of Frédéric Mistral, trans. by George Wickes. New York: New Directions Publishing, 1986.

More, Julian. *Views from a French Farmhouse*. Great Britain: Pavilion Books Limited, 1985; North Pomfret, Vermont: Trafalgar Square Publishing, 1992.

Pagnol, Marcel. *Jean de Florette* and *Manon of the Springs*. France: Editions Julliard, 1962; trans. by W. E. van Heyningen. New York: North Point Press, 1988.

———. *My Father's Glory and My Mother's Castle*. Great Britain: Hamish Hamilton, Ltd., 1960; reprint, trans. by Rita Barisse. New York: North Point Press, 1986.

Petrarch. *Selected Sonnets, Odes, and Letters*, edited by Thomas Goddard Bergin. Wheeling, Illinois: Harlan Davidson, Inc., 1966.

Design

Bredif, Josette. *Printed French Fabrics: Toiles de Jouy*. New York: Rizzoli, 1989.

Berenson, Kathryn. *Quilts of Provence: The Art and Craft of French Quiltmaking*. New York: Henry Holt and Company, Inc., 1996.

Campbell, Marian. *Decorative Ironwork*. New York: Harry N. Abrams, 1997.

Cootner, Cathryn M. *Anatolian Kilims*. London: Sotheby's Publications, Philip Wilson Publishers Ltd., 1990.

Dannenberg, Linda, Pierre LeVec, and Pierre Moulin. *Pierre Deux's Normandy: A French Country Style and Source Book*. New York: Clarkson N. Potter, Inc., 1988.

Geerlings, Gerald K. *Wrought Iron in Architecture: An Illustrated Survey*. New York: Charles Scribner's Sons; reprint, New York: Dover Publications, Inc., 1983.

Herbert, Tony, and Kathryn Huggins. *The Decorative Tile in Architecture and Interiors*. London: Phaidon Press, 1995.

Jackson, Mrs. F. Nevill. *Old Handmade Lace: With a Dictionary of Lace*. New York: Charles Scribner's Sons, 1900; reprint, Dover Publications, New York, 1987.

Karlson, Norman. *American Art Tile 1876–1941*. New York: Rizzoli, 1998.

Lebeau, Caroline. *Fabrics: The Decorative Art of Textiles*. New York: Clarkson N. Potter, Inc., 1994.

Marshall, Marlene Hurley. *Making Bits and Pieces Mosaics: Creative Projects for Home and Garden*. Pownal, Vermont: Storey Books, 1998.

Miller's Antiques Encyclopedia, edited by Judith Miller. London: Reed Consumer Books Limited, Ltd., 1998.

Moulin, Pierre, Pierre LeVec, and Linda Dannenberg. *Pierre Deux's French Country: A Style and Source Book*. New York: Clarkson N. Potter, Inc., 1984.

Niles, Bo. *Living with Lace*. New York: Stewart, Tabori & Chang, 1990.

Palliser, Mrs. Bury. *History of Lace*. New York: Charles Scribner's Sons, 1911; reprint, revised, rewritten, and enlarged by M. Jourdain and Alice Dryden. New York: Dover Publications, Inc., 1984.

Riley, Noel. *Tile Art: A History of Decorative Ceramic Tiles*. Secaucus, New Jersey: Chartwell Books, Inc., 1987.

Robertson, E. Graeme, and Joan Robertson. *Cast Iron Decoration: A World Survey*. New York: Thames and Hudson, Inc., 1994.

Van Lemmen, Hans. *Tiles: 1,000 Years of Architectural Decoration*. New York: Harry N. Abrams, Inc., 1993.

Wardle, Patricia. *Victorian Lace*. New York: Frederick A. Praeger, 1969.

Fairy Tales, Folk Tales, Philosophy

Bachelard, Gaston. *The Poetics of Space*. France: Presses Universitaires de France, 1958; foreword by John R. Stilgoe. Boston: Beacon Press, 1994.

Bettelheim, Bruno. *The Uses of Enchantment: The Meaning and Importance of Fairy Tales*. New York: Alfred A. Knopf, 1976; New York: Vintage Books, 1989.

Pourrat, Henri. *French Folktales.*, trans. and with an introduction by Royall Tyler. New York: Pantheon Books, 1989.

French Architecture

Boyer, Marie-France. *Really Rural: Authentic French Country Interiors*. London: Thames and Hudson Ltd., 1997.

Donald, Elsie Burch. *The French Farmhouse*. Great Britain: Little, Brown and Company, 1995.

Jacobs, Michael, and Hugh Palmer. *The Most Beautiful Villages of Provence*. New York: Thames and Hudson Ltd., 1994.

Lovatt-Smith, Lisa. *Provence Interiors*, edited by Angelika Muthesius. Germany: Taschen, 1996.

French Food and Cookbooks

Brennan, Georgeanne. *The Food and Flavors of Haute Provence*. San Francisco: Chronicle Books, 1997.

Brook, Stephen. *Oz Clarkes's Wine Companion: Southern France*. London: Webster's International Publishers, 1997.

Carrier, Robert. *Feasts of Provence*. New York: Rizzoli International Publications, Inc., 1992.

Chamberlain, Samuel. *Bouquet de France: An Epicurean Tour of the French Provinces*, trans. by Narcisse Chamberlain. New York: Gourmet Distributing Corp., 1952.

Christian, Glynn. *Edible France: A Traveler's Guide*, edited by Jenni Muir. New York: Interlink Books, 1997.

Duijker, Hubrecht. *Touring in the Wine Country: Provence*, edited by Hugh Johnson. Great Britain: Mitchell Beazley, 1998.

Freson, Robert. *The Taste of France*. New York: Stewart, Tabori & Chang, 1983.

Gilly, Antoine, and Jack Denton Scott. *Antoine Gilly's Feast of France*. New York: Thomas Y. Crowell Company, 1971.

Jacquelin, Louis, and René Poulain. *The Wines & Vineyards of France*, trans. by T. A. Layton. New York: G. P. Putnam's Sons, 1960.

Long, Dixon. *Markets of Provence*. New York: Collins Publishers Inc., 1996.

Olney, Richard. *Lulu's Provençal Table*. New York: HarperCollins Publishers, Inc., 1994.

————. *Provence: The Beautiful Cookbook*. San Francisco: Collins Publishers, 1993.

Vergé, Roger. *Roger Vergé's Entertaining in the French Style*. New York: Stewart, Tabori & Chang, Inc., 1986.

Gardens

Jones, Louisa. *Gardens in Provence*. Paris: Flammarion, 1992.

Taylor, Patrick. *The Garden Lover's Guide to France*. New York: Princeton Architectural Press, 1998.

Valery, Marie-Françoise. *Gardens in France*. Germany: Taschen, 1997.

Provence Guidebooks

Eyewitness Travel Guides. *Provence & the Côte d'Azur*. Main contributors, Roger Williams, Deni Bown. New York: DK Publishing, 1997.

Fodor's Exploring Provence. New York: Fodor's Travel Publications, Inc., 1998.

Heinic, Lionel. *Wonderful Provence*. France: Editions Ouest-France, 1993.

Knopf Guides. *Provence, France*. New York: Alfred A. Knopf, Inc., 1994.

Michelin Tourist Guide. *Provence*. France: Michelin et Cie, 1996.

Provence Lifestyle

Ardagh, John. *Rural France: The People, Places and Character of the Frenchman's France*. Salem, New Hampshire: Salem House, 1984.

Biehn, Michel. *Colors of Provence*, trans. by Rosanna M. Giammanco Frongia. New York: Stewart, Tabori & Chang, 1997.

Bentley, James. *To Live in France*. New York: Thames and Hudson Ltd., 1997.

Bullaty, Sonja, and Angelo Lomeo. *Provence*, text by Marie-Ange Guillaume. New York. Abbeville Press Publishers, 1993.

Conran, Terence, with Pierrette Pompon Bailhache and Maurice Croizard. *Terence Conran's France*. Boston: Little, Brown and Company, 1987.

Jones, Louisa. *Provence: A Country Almanac*. New York: Stewart, Tabori & Chang, 1993.

Silvester, Hans. *Lavender: Fragrance of Provence*, text by Christiane Meunier. New York: Harry N. Abrams, Inc., 1996.

Walden, Sara. *Provence: The Art of Living*, foreword by Terence Conran. New York: Stewart, Tabori & Chang, 1996.

ACKNOWLEDGMENTS

Heartfelt thanks to: Barb Fisher and Laura Chappell, talented artists, who collaborated so brilliantly on the murals and book illustrations; Keith Scott Morton, photographer, for our many years of association leading up to this book and for his sensitive photographs that imply the glowing light of Provence; Jacqueline Deval, my publisher and editor, for recognizing and clarifying the concepts of the illustrated cottage and for her enormous patience during the writing process; Virginia McRae and Christine Tanigawa, copy editors, for their incisive comments and corrections on the manuscript; Susi Oberhelman, art director, for her exquisite realization of the fairy-tale book design; Rachel Newman, editor emerita of *Country Living*, my mentor and dear friend who nurtured an extraordinary family of editors with courage and vision; Nancy Soriano, editor-in-chief of *Country Living*, for her encouragement and gifted eye; Mary Roby, Julio Vega, Rebecca Sawyer-Fay, Marjorie Gage, and Jessie Walker, additional friends at *Country Living*, who lent their support; Marcel Doyon, contractor, whose work on the cottage spanned four years and whose renovation of the carriage house inspires many; Al Johnson, for his help in constructing the carriage house; David Schultz, painter, for his meticulously executed decorative finishes and for his unfailingly courteous manner; Greg Fajardo, for his assistance with the finishes; Tom Ried and Rick Zoerb, for lighting up the cottage with a score of antique chandeliers; Bill Wood, Bob Wood, Wayne Winsand, Tim Kuffler, Arcinio Meza, and Mark Lansdon, for

Diane Row

Laura Chappell and Barb Fisher

Marné Harney and Max

special ironwork and carpentry; Diane Row, garden designer and unquestioned genius of the cottage garden; Marné Harney, gardener, for her faithful garden upkeep and for her sisterhood in the garden; Gene Motnyk, fabrications specialist, and Larry Horgan, landscape contractor, for beautifying the exterior; Alfredo Varela, Hilary Carlson, Lisa Steinke, and Jodie Katahara, for installing the garden and hardscape; Eloise Berg, Patti O'Neal, and Carla Talevi, for their dedicated assistance; photographers Michael Drejza and Katy Tartakoff, whose works enhance the cottage; Dana McCullough and Alyce Frank, painters, for their bravery with color; Sharon Lovejoy, for sharing her love of gardening; Anne Williams, John Ludwig, Harriett McMillan, Ruth Rogers Clausen, Cassandra Danz, Lauren Springer, Rob Proctor, and Rita and Steve Buchanan, for their erudition and taste in garden plants; Jimmie Cramer and Dean Johnson, designers, for making a fascinating world of their house and gardens; Paul Walker, whose insight gave me strength; antiques dealers Janice Woods, Eron Johnson, Bruno Hamon, and Barbara Thompson, who gave so generously of time, ideas, and antiques during my collecting and research; decorators, dealers, and friends Lyn Martin, Brooke Travelstead, Katherine Whitcomb, Carol Davis, Carolyn Sturges, Jennie Kurtz, Joan Grier, Jean Snow, Sally Starr, Martha Jones, Sara Rinehart, Elizabeth Schlosser, Tam O'Neill, Karen Moore, Jeffrey Moore, and Kent Choiniere, for their collective design eye, which influenced the myriad directions of the illustrated cottage; Jackie Burton, publicist, for her role in televising the cottage; Arnold Goldstein, who lent the name of his daughter, Séverine; Sylvia Tawse and Lyle Davis for introducing me to the cuisine of Lulu and Lucien Peyraud at Domaine Tempier; all the friends at Pasta, Pasta, Pasta, who offered fortifying repasts and enthusiasm; Tracey McCullough, and artists Sally McCullough and Cornelia Cottiati, for their astute creative guidance; Bill Sidley, whose unique gifts for words, romance, and associative thinking provided inspiration; Rachel and Ana Williams, for their fortitude during prolonged stretches of work and for their consent to live in a fantasy; Don and Lulu McCullough, whose passion for design and color became my own.

Rachel, Ana, and Niña Williams and Molly and Cookie

David Schultz, Greg Fajardo, Marcel Doyon, and Al Johnson

INDEX

A

Artistic traditions, 63
Atelier, 55–67
    chandelier, 56–57
    color scheme, 55–60
    mural, 55–60

B

Baguette bread, 37
Bessarabian kilim rug, 66
Botanical themes, 6, 60, 61, 63,
    64–65
Boudoir, 71–79
    chandeliers, 72–73, 76, 77
    defined, 74
    stairs to, 70, 71, 74

C

Carriage house, 83–99
    animals and, 86–88, 89
    chandelier, 92
    construction of, 89–95
    exterior, 96, 97, 98–99
    finishing, 95–97
    garage conversion, 83–86
    murals, 80, 83, 86, 87, 89
    theme of, 86–89
Ceramic tile. *See* Tile

Chandeliers, 48, 49, 78
    atelier, 56–57
    boudoir, 72–73, 76, 77
    carriage house, 92
    crystal, 78
    dining room, 34–35, 39
    kitchen, 44–45
Cottages, 37–39
Curtains
    cotton toile, 59
    lace, 20, 21, 39
    silk plaid, 59

D

Decorative objects, 37–39
Dining room, 33–39
    chandelier, 34–35, 39
    decorative objects, 37–39
    mural, 30, 32, 33, 34–35

E

Enamelware, 47

F

Fabrics
    cotton, 20, 59, 66
    dying, 66–67
    French, history of, 60–67
    hand-printed, 92, 93
    lace, 20, 21

    linen, 20
    silk, 20, 59, 66
Faux paint, 23
Finials, 92, 93, 94
Floor finishes
    pickled wood, 95–97
    whitewashed tile, 44–48
Flowers
    arrangements of, 28, 38, 39, 50,
      51, 60, 61, 78, 79
    garden, 105, 106–117
    still life, 63, 64–65
Fougasse bread, 37
Foyer, 11–15
    defined, 13
    mural, 8, 10, 11, 12, 13–14, 15
French breads, 37
French farmhouses, 13
French lace, 20
French tiles, 24
Furniture
    1920s French iron, 97, 118–119
    1920s wrought iron, 84–85
    19th century bed, 72–73
    19th century cupboard, 36, 37
    Baroque Revival chairs, 34–35
    Czech chest, 58, 59
    English mahogany chest, 28
    English, walnut chair, 58, 59–60
    French rosewood chair, 59–60
    Louis XIV chairs, 24, 26–27

G

Garage. *See* Carriage house
Garden, 103–119
  gate, 118
  patio, 118–119
  plant/color selection, 103–106
  Provençal, 110
  structural components, 106,
    107, 110
Garlic Rabbit, 51
Gibassier bread, 37
Grisaille, 22, 23

I

Ironworks, 94

K

Kitchen, 43–51
  atmosphere of, 43, 44–45
  chandelier, 44–45
  color coordination, 44–51
  dinnerware, 46, 47
  flooring, 44–48
  mural, 40, 42, 43

L

Lace
  curtains, 20, 21, 39
  history of, 20
  tambour, 20, 21
Larsson, Carl, 2
Lavender, 6, 11, 59
Limoges enamels, 47
Livestock, 88

M

Murals
  atelier, 55–60
  background of, 5–6
  carriage house, 80, 83, 86,
    87, 89
  dining room, 30, 32, 33, 34–35
  foyer, 8, 10, 11, 12, 13–14, 15
  kitchen, 40, 42, 43
  painters' method for, 20–24
  salon, 16, 18–19, 28, 29
  stair transition, 70, 71, 74

O

Old Paris porcelain, 24, 25, 28

P

Painters' method, 20–24
Painting techniques
  interior, distressed, 95–97
  trompe l'oeil, 1–2, 20–24, 97
Patio garden
  carriage house, 96, 97, 98–99
  main, 118–119
Perfumes, 75
Pillows, 48, 49, 59, 66
Piquer assiette, 23
Provençal cuisine
  Garlic Rabbit, 51
  overview, 50
  vineyards and, 38
Provençal gardens, 110
Provençal pottery, 34–35
Provençal themes, 6

R

Rugs, 66

S

Salon, 19–29
Soaps, 75
Studio. *See* Atelier

T

Textiles
  dying, 66–67
  history of, 60–67
Texture
  aged, distressed, 95–97
  mural, 33–37
Tile
  complimenting existing, 48–51
  French, 24
  whitewashing, 44–48
Trompe l'oeil
  defined, 1
  historical perspective, 1–2
  painters' method, 20–24
  symbolism of, 5–6
  texture and, 33–37

V

Vineyards, 38

W

Wines, 38